The Nature I found; The Me Nature found

James Allen

BookLeaf Publishing

Presentation by *BookLeaf Publishing*

Web: www.bookleafpub.com

E-mail: info@bookleafpub.com

ISBN: 9789357747042

First edition 2023

PREFACE

"I wandered lonely as a cloud
That floats on high o'er vales and hills,
When all at once I saw a crowd,
A host, of golden daffodils;
Beside the lake, beneath the trees,
Fluttering and dancing in the breeze.

Continuous as the stars that shine
And twinkle on the milky way,
They stretched in never-ending line
Along the margin of a bay:
Ten thousand saw I at a glance,
Tossing their heads in sprightly dance.

The waves beside them danced; but they
Out-did the sparkling waves in glee:
A poet could not but be gay,
In such a jocund company:
I gazed—and gazed—but little thought
What wealth the show to me had brought:

For oft, when on my couch I lie
In vacant or in pensive mood,
They flash upon that inward eye
Which is the bliss of solitude;
And then my heart with pleasure fills,
And dances with the daffodils."

- William Wordsworth

An Ode to What We Know

What we see, we understand,
But what takes flight may never land;
What we hear, we often crow,
But what we feel- is what we know.

We may drink from wisdom's flask
And cover up with stolid masks;
Should we shroud our joy or woe,
Still what we feel- is what we show.

Nature's simplicity goes on without end,
And yet, there are things, we can't comprehend;
We can't quite seem, to let it go,
Because what we feel- is what we know.

We conjure words to transcribe our thoughts,
It comes like thread and leaves in knots.
Seeds of love, we hope to sow,
For what we feel- is what we grow.

Words hold back what the heart can cry,
Through heart I feel, the urge to fly;
An emotion so pure, you could never bestow,
'Cause what we feel- is all we know . . .

Nature's Haiku: A Bird

I see ground and sky . . .
Yet I cannot seem to fly
The window is closed.

Water

Water,
All about the same;
The tides, the ponds, the oceans,
Evaporate to no name,
Remaining only, for as long as sun can hold . . .

The Giver's River

"I'm looking for something."
        "And what would that be?"
"I'm not quite sure."
        "You're lost, I see."
"I understand nothing."
        "But you understand me."
"Of that, I'm unsure."
        "But we seem to agree."

"Well, do you have an answer?"
        "Only one you might consider . . ."
"Tell me, I'll listen."
        "Then continue down the river."
"But what if that's disaster?"
        "Only then you'll see clearer."
"But do you have a reason?"
        "You can call me The Giver."

Transparent and Beautiful
Lively and blue
Smooth yet busy
Old yet new

"When should I stop?"
        "When you find a reason not to."
"Then will it ever end?"
        "Well that depends on you."

"I'm looking for something."
        "And what would that be?"
"I'm not quite sure."
        "You're lost, I see . . ."

The Tide Not Taken

The sky, the ocean, in deep black,
And shine does the moon in contrast;
A kindle of senses, awaiting unpack
With future in front, my past in back,
Alone in thought at last.

But where to go, I have no say
Of where the wind might blow tonight,
And though the rudder lies near on display,
I doubt if I will steer today,
Too fearful and weary for a fight;

A fight of the ocean that carries me so
For it has done me well 'till now,
But is this the life I wish to know;
Is this the best, path to go?
I sensed I had to choose but how?

I now will tell you, what I've learned,
But first, a question, you must consider;
Do you remember the ocean as it churned
Or rather the moon that glistened sunburned?
The answer should be natural, and come like a river.

To view the world in all its splendor,
Should you come across a choice long due,
There is no right or wrong contender,
Just try to recall and try to remember,
'The choice is yours, the choice is you.'

Reflections in the Pond

Quiet,
Tranquil even,
Yet I still can't seem to ignore
The sediments as they float around,
bounded by the edge while suspended above the floor.

How long shall I stay still in order to see
The transparent, clear, reflection of me.
Perhaps I never will;
Yet I remain,
Still.

Warmth
Embraces my skin
As the wind gently beckons;
A soft, but light melody;
A call from a bird that lasts for only seconds.

Near the pond I stand, confronted by identity;
I ponder what or who I am
Or what do people see,
And what makes me,
Me.

Alone,
I forge my path,
Not chosen by the sea,
But one filled with passion and insecurities
Of the things I could not change of nature's wrath.

And now the time has passed and I can take in
The crystal, clear water in front of me;
Is this reflection who I am or who I'm supposed to be?
Though nature never lies, except maybe by omission,
Inside us we'll find, our own crystal rendition.

Wind

Whispering quietly, and wisping away,
It carries and lifts up, up and away;
Never dismiss its gentle blow,
Don't just watch and let it go . . .

The Winter Wind Lie

Lost in the woods, I make my way
With winter snow packed near my knees;
With much spare time to throw away,
I sit and stare out at the trees.

The winter snow packed near my knees;
The winter wind biting at my tips;
I sit and stare out at the trees,
The air frosting from my lips.

The winter wind biting at my tips
As I contemplate my lie.
The air frosting from my lips,
Every time I sigh.

As I contemplate my lie.
I can't help but feel deceitful.
And every time I sigh,
To myself, I feel neglectful.

I can't help but feel deceitful
When I said that I was fine;
To myself I feel neglectful,
A fraudulent paradigm.

When I said that I was fine,
I was speaking from the wind.
A fraudulent paradigm
Where my roads of lies don't end.

I was speaking from the wind
As I stumbled on my fate.
Where my roads of lies don't end
And entraps me in this state.

As I stumbled on my fate,
It pulled me away from everybody,
And entrapped me in this state,
this dreaded state of melancholy.

It pulled me away from everybody
And I still yet don't know why
this dreaded state of melancholy
Never lets me cry.

Tears of the Wind:
A Saunter through a Lonesome Town

Here I stand in this lonesome town
I suppose, pulled in by the wind;
I wander this little town alone,
Deciding which path to walk.
This is how I will spend my day
As tumbleweeds dance in the air.

With each passing step I take in this torrid air,
I start to learn a fragment more, about this little old town.
I can close my eyes and picture them living day to day
And the many travelers that were drawn by the same alluring wind.
This town has several faded paths to walk,
But I guess I'll have to walk them all alone.

I wonder how this town must feel with it being left alone,
With no one left to stay and breathe its firewood air;
The paths left void and forgotten of a human's walk.
But the more I walk within this lonesome town,
The more I feel distracted by its wind,
And the more the sun reveals the passing of the day.

I wonder if this place will remember today,
After I'm gone and it's left again alone.
It'll probably bring more friends from the wind,
To also breathe its cinnamon dry air;
But for now I sit amidst this quiet town,
Jotting down this poem as I walk.

This town is old, yet has such lovely paths to walk.
I'll leave some paths untrodden, and for another day;
I reckon one day I'll revisit, this lonesome, voiceless town,
And walk its paths again, alone.
I take another breath of this now sultry air
And enjoy my final steps, guided by its wind.

I have no eloquent words to describe this special wind;
This wind that loops and beckons as I walk.
Maybe it changes with the air
Or with the passing of the day;
I can tell it cries when it's alone,
This once lively town.

I wonder if the wind, knew to blow today.
I wonder if it knew I walked alone.
Until I breathe this air again, the air of this lonesome town . . .

Leaving behind the sound of the wind...

Leaving behind the sound of the wind,
A boy sets off on a journey.
A journey to awaken
And remember once more
His true inner voice;
So fleeting, yet
Evermore.
Farewell,
Wind.

Ground

Grass and flowers grow, and spread like a fire
Reaching far and wide,
Out through the land and stretching higher
Upwards toward the sky with glee.
Never have I seen such art
Done so perfectly . . .

For The Love of Flowers

Flowers make our life more beautiful. They paint the various ground around us while never letting up on its power to astound us. They come in many shapes and many sizes to discover while you stroll. Some you can eat, while some can soothe the skin. Some heal the body, while others heal the soul. Each flower has a deeper meaning that speaks to the heart, but when they are together is when they start to make art.

In the morning as I walk through my garden, my senses are enlivened with vibrant colors and the fragrances that surround me. Each one is gifted with its own personality, its own charm, as I'm held captive by their beauty. All flowers have something to show, but the love of flowers is to help them grow.

For the love of flowers is a reminder to us all, to appreciate the simple beauty that surrounds us all.

> A flower, unique;
> Yet through earth they learn to speak.
> One word, elegance . . .

The Heart's Arboretum:
To Grow a Heart to Care

A Tree;
They bring life to thee;
Yet how do they live so peacefully sound
With all their roots spread throughout the ground?
They seem to do so many things, yet somehow they need me.
A tree will never lie or steal or abuse the things they do.
They take our toxic, exhaled air and breathe life back into you.
They give you shade and block the wind when nature has its way.
How many times have you walked out and thanked a tree today
For providing wood and creatures' homes and taking care of you?
But one may say they have no thought, why is it our concern?
But the thanks we say is not only for the tree, but for us to learn.
The tree is there for us to use and use it as we will,
But never overreach, overuse, and overkill.
They supply, yet expect nothing in return.
Always there;
Forever fair;
Here to stay,
And to care.
The people,
The things,
And the joy
Sun brings;
Often took
For granted,
It seems . . .
Remember to take the time, to thank the things we love and share.
For only then our heart, will truly learn to care.

My Garden of Moms

I live in a Garden of Moms;
They hear my every qualm.
They feed & heal
And bring joy, what a deal!
Yes, my Garden of Chrysanthemoms.

Fire

Finding emotion and response
In things big and small,
Radiating a fiery passion throughout
Everything, Everywhere, All at Once . . .

Bravery in the Flame

A kindling awaits patiently to ignite into a name.
As the tinder rises gradually and begins to float into the air,
Rise to find bravery, hidden in the flame.

As we look into the silver, yet clear and polished frame,
There awaits many emotions, some too deep to compare;
A kindling awaits patiently to ignite into a name.

Some tend to find themselves chasing after fame
While others tend to fall, and stumble into despair.
Rise to find bravery, hidden in the flame.

To learn to fight aloud, and to set aside shame;
To those who are lost, with eyes that seem beyond repair;
A kindling awaits patiently to ignite into a name.

A multitude of names, though none ever the same,
And each with their own, very distinct flare;
Rise to find bravery, hidden in the flame.

A fire burns passionately, with no need to tame;
It sits within all of us, and the things we learn to bear.
A kindling awaits patiently to ignite into a name;
Rise to find bravery, hidden in the flame.

Breathe into Fire

Just relax
Just breathe
Breathe in
Breathe out
Out of sight
Out of mind
Mind your decisions
Mind your thoughts
Thoughts seep
Thoughts grow
Grow your Mind
Grow your heart
Heart of gold
Heart attack
Attack on me
Attack of panic
Panic attack
Panic at the disco
Disco lights
Disco music
Music to relax
Music to calm
Calm your nerves
Calm down

Down the street
Down the rabbit hole
Hole of fear
Hole of doubt
Doubt of my future
Doubt of myself
Myself I see
Myself to be
Be present
Be better
Better safe than sorry
Better late than never
Never-ending
Never look back
Back to a better me
Back to reality
Reality TV
Reality check
Check in
Check out
Out of wood
Out of fire
Fire and Ice
Fire that is just
Just . . .
Breathe . . .

The Seared Fragments of a Beautiful Fallen Ballad

I hear a faint song of April,
A song no one can copy;
As my eyes envision flowers,
A field of Opium Poppy.

The raven echos through the hall,
Yet I still weep alone;
Family and acquaintances gather 'round,
Still my body feels of stone.

The raven echos through the hall,
Yet not the hall I'm in;
Family and acquaintances gather 'round
For the interment to begin

I hear a faint song of April,
One I seem to know;
As my eyes envision flowers,
And my heart begins to grow.

I never meant to cry,
Yet I still weep alone.
The hours arduously passing by,
Still my body feels of stone.

I never meant to cry,
For that's not what she would want?
The hours arduously passing by
As a now vague figure seems to haunt.

A ballad for the eyes,
A song no one can copy,
While near my feet lies
A field of Opium Poppy.

'Twas it fate, or a curse?'
That leaves me here to lie;
For I would like to know
Before I finish my goodbye.

'Twas it fate, or a curse?'
That burns me up inside;
For I would like to know:
'Where does my frustration reside?'

A ballad for the eyes,
Too beautiful to forget,
While near my feet lies
Many pieces left to get.

It must have been a curse
That leaves me here to lie;
For fate would never leave
Before I finish my goodbye.

It must have been a curse,
A cruel curse at that;
For fate would never leave
My heart so torn and cracked.

I hear a faint song of April,
Too beautiful to forget,
Yet I still feel a flame,
That burns me with regret.

A painful, sorrowful cry;
A truth I dare accept;
Out of all the things we shared,
This smile is what I kept.

A painful, sorrowful cry;
And a truth I *must* accept.
Out of all the things we shared,
Her smile is *all* I kept.

I hear a faint song of April,
A song no one can copy;
As my eyes envision flowers,
A field of Opium Poppy.

Sky

Skies above, skies afar, making nature glad;
Keeping dreams afloat,
You never knew you had . . .

Rosely Colored Rain

Oh how the rain falls swiftly from the sky,
The sky that once blew clouds and summer breeze.
In bliss I'd be, if only I could fly
And soar above the crown atop the trees.

I stand and watch the rain observantly
To see the things that most can not discern;
The rain, it speaks so universally,
Yet paints the sky and feeds the golden fern.

They try to say the color is a blue,
But I see love like petals of a rose;
They say it's not a rosely tinted hue,
But what I see is love that falls and flows.

Though others speak they do not see the same,
Still all I see . . .   is rosely colored rain.

A Forgotten Dream of Sky

This weather is bleak, and my hands are getting brittle;
How long has it been?
Ten? . . . No twenty minutes? Give or take a little?
Will this train ever arrive?
I have things to do and rest to get,
Let alone, survive.

Hmm? What's this?
A person I didn't notice before?
I shouldn't look too long;
Just a quick glance will do;
Wow, he's just a young one,
And in old and tattered shoes.

His pants are similarly battered,
And his jacket's small as well;
Are his parents nearby? Or someone I should tell?
He must be tired too;
He must have a story I bet-

But wait, his eyes . . .
How come they strike me so?
Maybe I'll follow his glance, to find out where they go;
They seem up and lost, and into the night sky;
They seem to glisten and radiate in amusement, not woe.

Up in the stars, they appear to be,
His eyes make me reminisce, to a younger version of me,
A me that could dream and get lost in a journey.
		Where did that me go?
		And when did he leave?
Maybe when I grew up and began to disbelieve.

I miss the ambition, and the passion in the soul;
I wish to travel to the stars, and never to get old.

Everyone wants to believe in something;
But as they grow older,
they seem to find that they can't anymore . . .
So they pretend that they cannot hear that inner cry
Until eventually,
they can no longer hear that it's saying to fly . . .

I want the stars to shine,
		and to fill my head again;
I want you, I plead,
		to let me dream again.

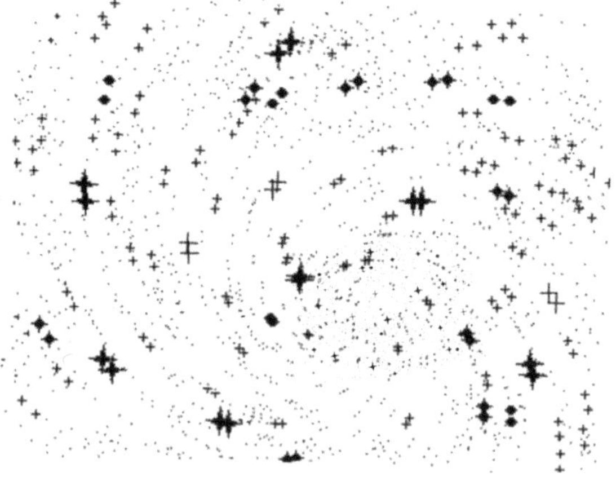

Where Dreams Take Flight

I look at the sky as birds flutter by and notice how high the birds reach, but why? Maybe they're too shy to see eye to eye or to bid the heavens a parting goodbye. I feel like humans are in some ways the same; we feel like a personage, that's been fitted to a frame. We wish to watch the wisping leaves, but the sky was not our aim. Sure, we may make ways to fly, but the sky we'll never claim.

Sky is filled with dreams

Boundlessly floating in mist;

Yes dreams in the sky . . .

Nature's Cento: An Open Window

I'm looking for something
Too beautiful to forget;
A journey to awaken,
Myself to be . . .

Near the pond I stand, confronted by identity;
A kindling awaits patiently to ignite into a name,
Upwards toward the sky with glee;
But the sky we'll never claim-

The tides, the ponds, the oceans,
I suppose, pulled in by the wind;
Oh how the rain falls swiftly from the sky
And I still yet don't know why . . .

Everyone wants to believe in something;
Don't just watch and let it go.
They bring life to thee,
Radiating a fiery passion throughout-

To view the world in all its splendor:
Skies above, skies afar, making nature glad;
Yes, my Garden of Chrysanthemoms,
A flower, unique.

I see ground and sky . . .
Through heart I feel,   the urge to fly.

The Nature I found; The Me Nature found

The Nature I found
While I drift throughout the trees
The me Nature found
As it beckons through the leaves
peacefully waiting for me . . .